The World's Deadliest EPIDEMICS

Claire Henry

PowerKiDS press

New York

Published in 2014 by The Rosen Publishing Group, Inc.
29 East 21st Street, New York, NY 10010

First Edition

Produced for Rosen by Cyan Candy, LLC
Editor: Joshua Shadowens
Designer: Erica Clendening, Cyan Candy

Photo Credits: Cover, pp. 5, 9, 10, 11, 12, 13, 14 Shutterstock.com; pp. 4, 23 Hinochika/
Shutterstock.com; p. 8 PD-USA, via Wikimedia Commons; p. 15 Jeffrey Gluck, via Wikimedia
Commons; p. 16 Otis Historical Archives Nat'l Museum of Health & Medicine, via Wikimedia
Commons; p. 17 USAID U.S. Agency for International Development, via Wikimedia Commons;
pp. 18 , 19, 21 Wikimedia Commona; p. 20 Cynthia Goldsmith, via Wikimedia Commons; p. 22
(bottom) courtesy of the National Museum of Health and Medicine, Armed Forces Institute
of Pathology, Washington, D.C., United States, via Wikimedia Commons; p. 22 (top) Harris &
Ewing photographers, via Wikimedia Commons; p. 24 Nathan Holland/Shutterstock.com; p. 25
Centers for Disease Control and Prevention, via Wikimedia Commons; p. 26 Rosser1954, via
Wikimedia Commons; p. 30 Frontpage/Shutterstock.com.

Library of Congress Cataloging-in-Publication Data

Henry, Claire, 1975–
 The world's deadliest epidemics / by Claire Henry. — First edition.
    pages cm — (The world's deadliest)
 Includes index.
 ISBN 978-1-4777-6157-1 (library) — ISBN 978-1-4777-6158-8 (pbk.) —
 ISBN 978-1-4777-6159-5 (6-pack)
 1. Epidemics—Juvenile literature. 2. Communicable diseases—Juvenile literature. I. Title.
 RA653.5.H46 2014
 614.4—dc23
                              2013029564

Manufactured in the United States of America

CPSIA Compliance Information: Batch #W14PK8: For Further Information contact Rosen Publishing, New York, New York at 1-800-237-9932

TABLE OF CONTENTS

DEADLY DISEASES

Do you remember the last time you were sick with a cold or the flu? You may have taken some medicine, rested for a few days, and then felt better. While some illnesses are not very dangerous to humans, others can be incredibly deadly!

Many diseases, such as the flu, are caused by **viruses**. Some viruses are spread through the air, and others through contact with an infected surface. When a large number of people in a certain area all catch the same sickness, it is called an **epidemic**.

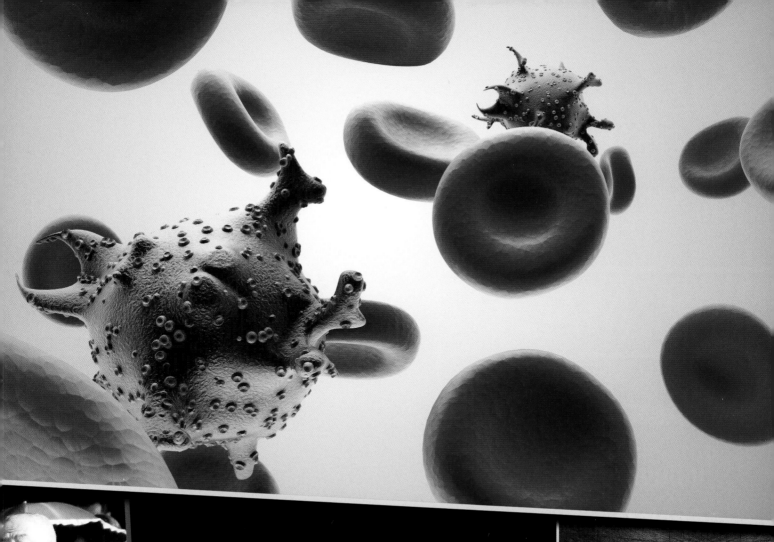

Above: The HIV virus attacks blood cells.
Left: These people are wearing face masks to stop the spread of influenza.

Epidemics that spread over much larger areas are also called **pandemics**. AIDS, for example, is considered a pandemic. This is because it has affected millions of people all across the world. About 35 million people have died since the disease was discovered in 1981.

For most of human history, people had very few ways to fight diseases. Today, many dangerous sicknesses can be prevented with vaccines. The first vaccine was developed in the late 1700s to fight a devastating illness called smallpox. Before the vaccine, smallpox

MAJOR EPIDEMICS

NAME	DATE
Influenza/H1N1/Swine Flu	2009–2010
Cholera	2010–2011
Cholera	2008–2009
Meningitis	2009–2010
Severe Acute Respiratory Syndrome (SARS)	2002–2003
Hand, Foot, and Mouth Disease	2010
Dengue Fever	2011–present
Dengue Fever	2006
Hepatitis B	2009
Ebola	2012

killed hundreds of thousands each year. By the late 1970s, smallpox had been **eradicated**, or completely gotten rid of. While smallpox is no longer a threat, many other epidemics still occur around the world each year!

2000–PRESENT

LOCATION	DEATHS
worldwide	18,500–575,000+
Haiti	6,500+
Zimbabwe	4,293
West Africa	931
Asia	775
China	537
Pakistan	350+
India	50+
India	49
Central Africa	48

PLAGUE: THE BLACK DEATH

The Black Death was an outbreak of sickness that swept through Europe in the Middle Ages. Some cases of the illness were caused by **pneumonic plague**. This type of plague affected peoples' lungs. Most of the cases, though, were **bubonic plague**. Bubonic plague causes high fevers and swollen **lymph nodes**.

Plague is caused by **bacteria**. Bacteria are tiny living things that cannot be seen with the eye alone. In the Middle Ages, the plague was spread when rats infected by the bacteria were bitten by fleas. The fleas then bit humans and passed the bacteria to them.

Left: The Catholic Church was a large part of peoples' lives in the Middle Ages. Many looked to priests to heal them from the plague.
Right: In Christianity, plagues have often been thought of as punishment from God.

MIDDLE AGES

The Middle Ages were a period of European history lasting from about AD 500 to around 1500. Life in the Middle Ages was very different than today. Homes had no running water and human waste was often dumped in rivers. These conditions helped diseases spread quickly, especially in crowded cities.

BLACK DEATH IN EUROPE

The **medieval** epidemic began in Asia and arrived in Europe around 1347. It is believed that about 25–30 million people died during the Black Death. That was one-third of Europe's population at the time!

EFFECT ON EUROPE

The Black Death had a major effect on medieval Europe. In some places, over 80 percent of the population died and entire villages were wiped out. With fewer workers, wages rose, but so did the cost of goods. Some people were upset that God and their Church had not stopped the plague. Many people looked to science to explain the plague, leading to the beginnings of modern medicine.

This sixteenth-century church is called Capela dos Ossos, or Chapel of Bones. It is believed that some of the bones may belong to people who died in the Black Death.

Many people saw the plague as the work of God. Others believed it could be explained by science.

THE PLAGUE TODAY

You may be surprised to learn that the bubonic plague is still around today. There are about seven cases in the United States each year, mostly in western states. Most cases can be easily treated with medicines called **antibiotics**.

MALARIA:
THE MOSQUITO MENACE

Malaria is a very deadly disease caused by a parasite. Parasites are tiny living things that live in or on another living thing. Malaria is spread when a female mosquito infected with the parasite bites a human. The parasite is passed to the human through the mosquito's saliva. Once the parasites are inside a person's body, they grow and reproduce in the body's red blood cells.

About 7 to 30 days after being bitten, people infected with malaria begin to have high fevers and chills. People with very severe, or bad, cases of malaria may have seizures, develop kidney failure, go into a coma, or even die.

Many people use fogging to kill mosquitoes.

MOSQUITOES

A mosquito is a type of fly. There are about 3,000 different types of mosquitoes. However, only three types are responsible for spreading deadly diseases, such as malaria, dengue fever, and the West Nile virus. Diseases spread by mosquitoes kill about 2 million people a year!

MALARIA DEATH TOLL

There are over 200 million cases of malaria around the world each year. About 660,000 people **diagnosed** with malaria die, though the actual number of deaths may be much higher. About 90 percent of malaria deaths occur in Africa and 86 percent of those who die are children.

PREVENTION AND TREATMENT

Today, there is no malaria vaccine. However, there are drugs that can lessen the chance someone will get malaria. Malaria can also be treated and cured with certain medicines. Unfortunately, many people who get malaria live in poorer areas and do not have access to these medicines.

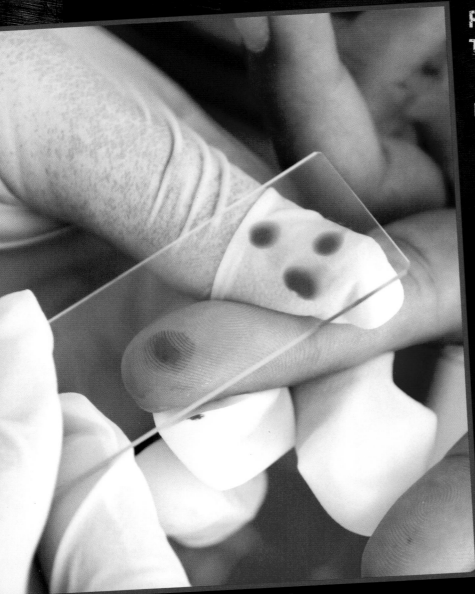

A blood test can show whether someone is infected with malaria parasites.

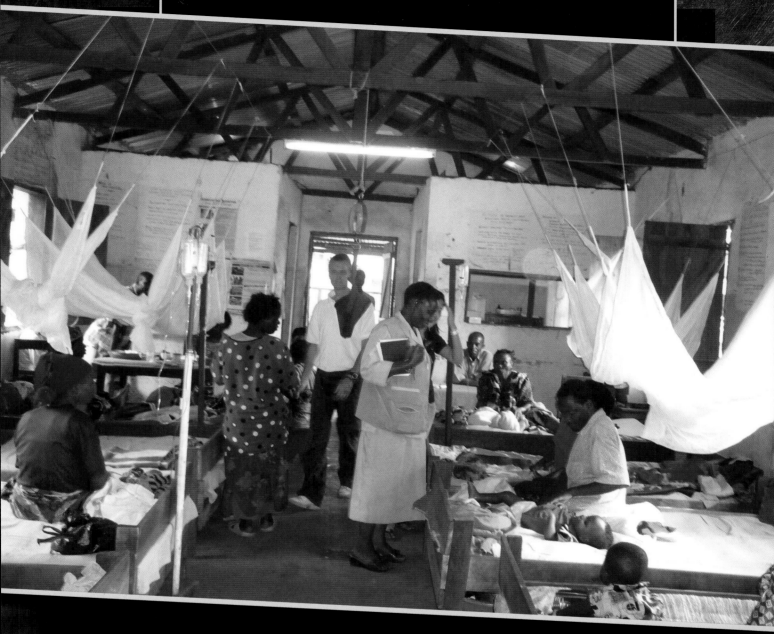

This clinic in Tanzania treats people who have been infected with malaria. Most of those who die from the disease are children.

NOTHING BUT NETS

One of the best ways to stop the spread of malaria is with mosquito nets. When nets are placed over beds, they protect people from bites while they are sleeping. The UN Foundation's Nothing But Nets campaign has sent over 7 million nets to Africa since 2006.

TUBERCULOSIS: THE WASTING DISEAS

Tuberculosis, or TB, is a disease that usually affects a person lungs. It is caused by bacteria. When an infected person coughs sneezes, the bacteria is released into the air. When other peopl breathe in the bacteria, they become infected, too.

Many people infe with the tuberculos bacteria do not bec sick. Their bodies are able to fight th bacteria and they cannot spread it tc others. However, people who becon infected get sick just a few weeks. may get a bad co fever, and chills. often lose a lot o weight and may cough up blood.

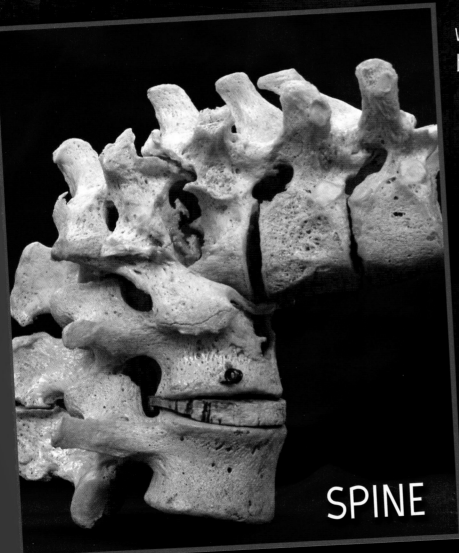

SPINE

This photo shows a person's spine that has collapsed because of tuberculosis infection.

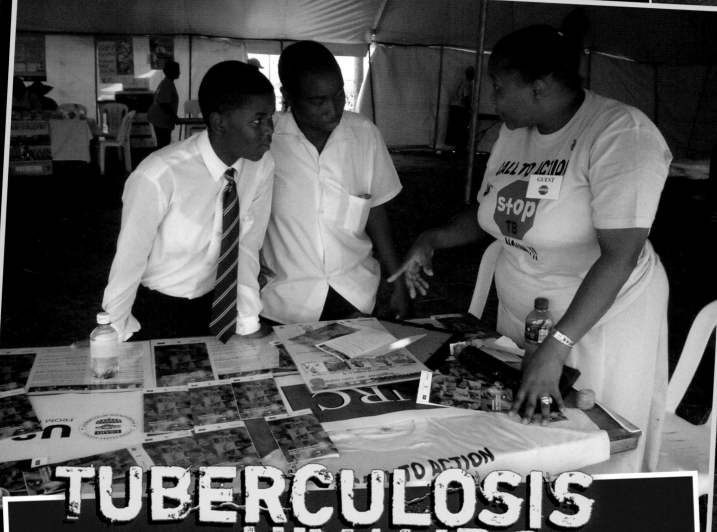

TUBERCULOSIS AND HIV/AIDS

The **immune system** is the part of the body that fights illness. A person with a healthy immune system is often able to fight the tuberculosis bacteria. HIV and AIDS, however, make a person's immune system weaker. Tuberculosis is the biggest killer of people with HIV and AIDS.

TUBERCULOSIS THROUGH HISTORY

Cases of tuberculosis have been recorded for as long as humans have been writing down history. There is even evidence of tuberculosis in Egyptian mummies! Today, almost 9 million cases of tuberculosis are diagnosed each year, and about 1.4 million people will die. Over 95 percent of these deaths occur in poor and developing countries, such as India, Vietnam, and Nigeria.

TB TESTS

Tuberculosis testing can be done by either a skin test or a blood test. Skin tests are often done on children before they begin going to school. These tests help stop the spread of tuberculosis by catching it early and treating it before a person gets sick.

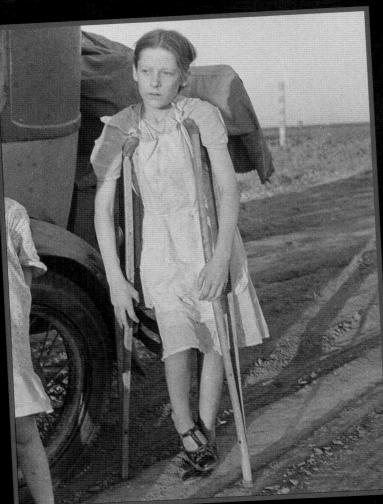

While tuberculosis often affects the lungs, it can also affect a person's bones, as it has in this girl.

Meriwether Jeff Thompson, a famous brigadier general in the Civil War, was infected with tuberculosis and died in 1876. About 13,000 Civil War soldiers died from tuberculosis during the war.

TREATMENT

Tuberculosis can be cured by taking four different medicines for 6–12 months. In some parts of the world where TB is very common, people use a vaccine to prevent infection.

INFLUENZA: NO ORDINARY FLU

Today, many people think of influenza, or the flu, as not very dangerous. However, a type of influenza was actually responsible for the deadliest epidemic in recorded history! Influenza is caused by a virus. The influenza virus affects the parts of the body that help in breathing, called the **respiratory system**.

The flu is a **contagious** disease. This means it can be spread from person to person. This most often happens when an infected person sneezes or coughs and another person breathes in the virus. People can also catch the flu by touching infected surfaces and then touching their mouths or noses.

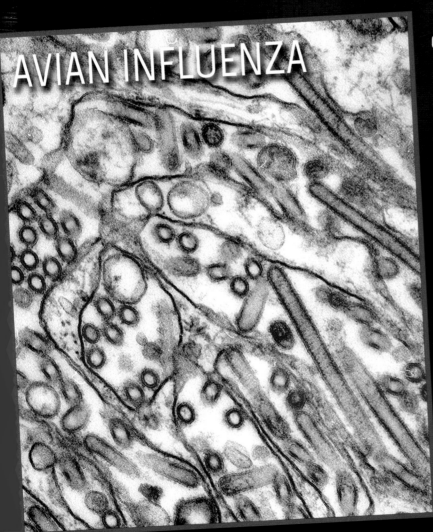

AVIAN INFLUENZA

This colored electron micrograph shows the H5N1 influenza, or avian flu, virus close up.

SPANISH FLU OF 1918

In 1918 a new type of flu spread through much of the world. The Spanish Flu could kill people in less than a day. Scientists believe the flu killed by turning the body's immune system against itself. Peoples' lungs filled with fluids and they were not able to get any oxygen.

SPANISH FLU EFFECTS

Between 1918 and 1919, the Spanish Flu killed about 50 million people around the world, including 675,000 people in the United States. The Spanish Flu killed more people than the Black Death and World War I. Between 20 percent and 40 percent of the world's population became sick. The flu was most deadly to people between the ages of 20 and 50 years old. This was unusual because influenza is generally more dangerous to children and the elderly.

Above:
This photo shows part of the flu ward at Walter Reed Hospital, in Washington, D.C.
Right: Emergency military hospitals, such as the one seen here at Camp Funston, in Kansas, were quickly set up to take care of the sick.

By June 2009, the swine flu had spread around the world. These people in Japan wear face masks to protect themselves.

OTHER INFLUENZA EPIDEMICS

There have been three other influenza epidemics since 1918, though none have been as deadly. Between 1957–1958, the Asian Flu killed about 69,800 people in the United States and around 2 million worldwide. In 1968–1969 the Hong Kong Flu killed around 33,800 people. In 2009–2010, between 43 million and 89 million people were infected by the HINI virus, called the swine flu, and hundreds of thousands may have died.

CHOLERA: DANGER IN THE WATER

Cholera is caused by a type of bacteria that infects the intestines. Most people who are infected with cholera will have mild symptoms or no symptoms at all. In some people, though, the disease causes a lot of pain in a person's stomach, diarrhea, and vomiting. People with severe cholera symptoms can lose a lot of their bodies' fluids, and they can die within hours.

The bacteria that cause cholera are often found in **contaminated** water and food. The disease can spread quickly in places where the drinking water comes into contact with sewage, or human waste.

Cholera is often spread in parts of Africa where there isn't access to clean drinking water.

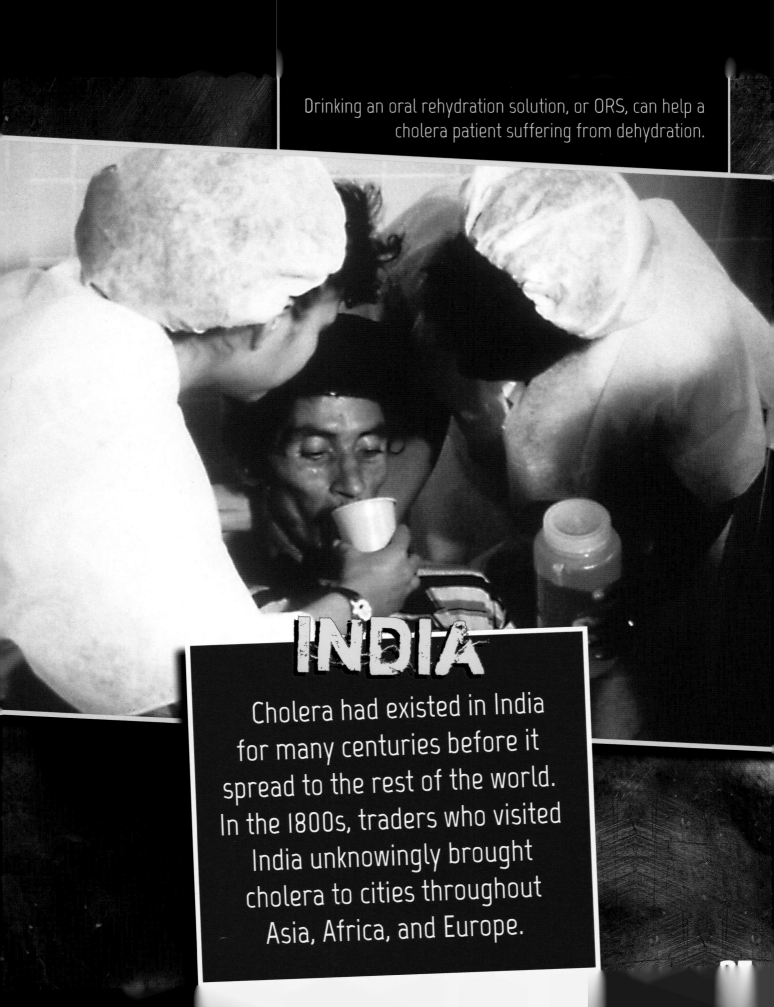

Drinking an oral rehydration solution, or ORS, can help a cholera patient suffering from dehydration.

INDIA

Cholera had existed in India for many centuries before it spread to the rest of the world. In the 1800s, traders who visited India unknowingly brought cholera to cities throughout Asia, Africa, and Europe.

AIR OR WATER?

When cholera first began to spread, people thought the disease was caused by bad air. In the mid-nineteenth century, the link between cholera and contaminated water was discovered. People worked to clean their cities and create clean water supplies.

THE SEVENTH PANDEMIC

Since the nineteenth century, there have been seven major cholera pandemics. The current pandemic began in South Asia in 1961. Today, there are about 3 million to 5 million cases of cholera each year and around 100,000 deaths.

SACRED
TO THE MEMORY OF THOSE INHABITANTS
WHO DIED FROM CHOLERA
DURING THE EPIDEMIC OF 1832
AND ARE HERE INTERRED

This plaque in Kilmarnock, Scotland, memorializes those who died in an 1832 cholera epidemic.

MALARIA AROUND THE WORLD

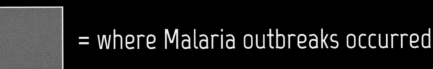

NORTH AMERICA

Atlantic Ocean

EUROPE

ASIA

AFRICA

Indian Ocean

SOUTH AMERICA

Pacific Ocean

AUSTRALIA

= where Malaria outbreaks occurred

DEADLIEST EPIDEMICS

Here is a list of the deadliest epidemics and pandemics in recorded history. You will find descriptions of many of the illnesses listed in the pages of this book. You can read more about the other illnesses on this list in books and on the Internet.

DEADLIEST EPIDEMICS

ILLNESS	CAUSE
Tuberculosis	bacteria
Spanish Flu	virus
Bubonic Plague/Black Death	bacteria
Malaria	parasite
Smallpox	virus
Cholera	bacteria
Yellow Fever	virus
HIV/AIDS	virus
Typhus	bacteria
Polio	virus

EPIDEMIC TYPHUS

Typhus is caused by bacteria and spread by body lice. It is often called Camp Fever because it spreads quickly through large groups of people living in cramped, dirty conditions. Typhus killed 10 million people during the Thirty Years' War and another 3 million in Russia, Poland, and Romania during World War I.

IN HISTORY

LOCATION OF MAJOR OUTBREAKS	DEATH TOLL
Developing countries worldwide	1.4–2 million per year
worldwide	50 million
Europe/Asia	25–30 million
Sub-Saharan Africa/tropical climates	660,000–1.2 million per year
North and South America/worldwide	60 million Native Americans
India/South Asia/Haiti	100,000 per year
North America/South America/Africa	30,000 per year
worldwide	35 million
Europe/worldwide	10 million
worldwide	3,000 deaths

Note—It is not always possible to know the exact number of people killed by a certain disease during a certain epidemic. Many epidemics occurred before diseases were fully understood and before accurate records were kept. There are also often no official start or end dates for epidemics. In this book, we have made every effort to use the most reliable and widely accepted numbers available.

STOPPING THE SPREAD

Epidemics have had a major effect on human history. They have wiped out entire villages and cultures and changed the way people live. While many diseases have been cured or can be easily prevented with medicines, many others still claim thousands of lives each year. By understanding the causes of history's worst epidemics, we may be able to stop the spread of these deadly diseases and others like them in the future!

Early testing and vaccinations are two of the best ways to prevent the spread of dangerous diseases.

eye alone. Some bacteria cause illness or rotting, but others are helpful.

bubonic plague (boo-BAH-nik PLAYG) The most common form of plague in humans, characterized by fever, delirium, and the formation of buboes.

contagious (kun-TAY-jus) Able to be passed on.

contaminated (kun-TA-mih-nay-tid) To make something unusable by adding poisons to it.

diagnosed (dy-ig-NOHSD) To figure out problems by looking at the signs.

epidemic (eh-pih-DEH-mik) The quick spreading of a sickness so that many people have it at the same time.

eradicated (ee-ra-duh-KAYT-ed) When something has been gotten rid of.

immune system (ih-MYOON SIS-tum) The system that keeps the body safe from sicknesses.

lymph nodes (LIMPF NOHDZ) A number of small swellings in the lymphatic system where lymph is filtered and lymphocytes are formed.

pandemic (pan-DEH-mik) Occurring over a wide geographic area and affecting an exceptionally high proportion of the population.

pneumonic plague (noo-MOH-nik PLAYG) A contagious bacterial disease characterized by fever, delirium, and sometimes infection of the lungs.

respiratory system (RES-puh-ruh-tor-ee SIS-tem) The parts of the body that help in breathing.

vaccines (vak-SEENZ) A shot that keeps a person from getting a certain sickness.

viruses (VY-rus-iz) Tiny things that cause a disease.

INDEX

WEBSITES

Due to the changing nature of Internet links, PowerKids Press has developed
an online list of websites related to the subject of this book. This site is updated
regularly. Please use this link to access the list:
www.powerkids.com/twd/epidem/